GRADE

Success With

Reading Comprehension

SCHOLASTIC

Editor: Ourania Papacharalambous
Cover design by Tannaz Fassihi; cover illustration by Kevin Zimmer
Interior design by Cynthia Ng
Interior illustrations by Stephen Brown (9–10, 12, 15–16, 18–21, 26–27, 33, 35, 37, 40–42); Doug Jones (spot art)
Icons: The Noun Project (19, 21); all other images © Shutterstock.com

ISBN 978-1-338-79858-6
Scholastic Inc., 557 Broadway, New York, NY 10012
Copyright © 2022 Scholastic Inc.
All rights reserved. Printed in the U.S.A.
First printing, January 2022
1 2 3 4 5 6 7 8 9 10   40 29 28 27 26 25 24 23 22

INTRODUCTION

Parents and teachers alike will find *Scholastic Success With Reading Comprehension* to be a valuable educational tool. It is designed to help students in the first grade improve their reading comprehension skills. The practice pages incorporate puzzles and other fun activities that keep children engaged as they improve their comprehension skills. Children will practice finding the main idea, reading for details, drawing conclusions, and following directions. They are also challenged to develop vocabulary, identify cause and effect, and analyze characters. On page 4, you will find a list of the key skills covered in the activities throughout this book. Practicing and reviewing these important reading skills will help children become better readers. Remember to praise children for their efforts and successes!

TABLE OF CONTENTS

Grade-Appropriate Skills Covered in *Scholastic Success With Reading Comprehension: Grade 1*

Ask and answer questions about key details in a text.

Retell stories, including key details, and demonstrate understanding of their central message or lesson.

Describe characters, settings, and major events in a story, using key details.

Use illustrations and details in a story to describe its characters, setting, or events.

Identify the main topic and retell key details of a text.

Ask and answer questions to help determine or clarify the meaning of words and phrases in a text.

Distinguish between information provided by pictures or other illustrations and information provided by the words in a text.

Use the illustrations and details in a text to describe its key ideas.

Demonstrate understanding of the organization and basic features of print.

Recognize the distinguishing features of a sentence.

Know and apply grade-level phonics and word analysis skills in decoding words.

Recognize and read grade-appropriate irregularly spelled words.

Read with sufficient accuracy and fluency to support comprehension.

Demonstrate command of the conventions of standard English grammar and usage when writing or speaking.

Print all upper- and lowercase letters.

Use sentence-level context as a clue to the meaning of a word or phrase.

Use context to confirm or self-correct word recognition and understanding, rereading as necessary.

Sort words into categories to gain a sense of the concepts the categories represent.

Define words by category and by one or more key attributes.

Identify real-life connections between words and their use.

Trucks

**Read about trucks.
Then follow the directions below.**

> The **main idea** tells us what the whole story is about.

Trucks do important work. Dump trucks carry away sand and rocks. Cement trucks have a barrel that turns round and round. They deliver cement to workers who are making sidewalks. Fire trucks carry water hoses and firefighters. Gasoline is delivered in large tank trucks. Flat bed trucks carry wood to people who are building houses.

1 What is the main idea of the paragraph? Write it in the circle below.

2 Draw a line from the main idea to the trucks described in the paragraph.

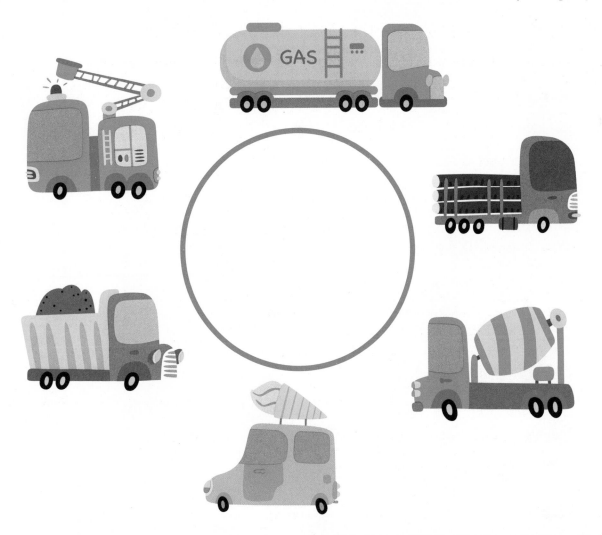

Acrobats

Today, I went to the county fair. My favorite part of the fair was the acrobats. Acrobats can do great things. An acrobat named Priscilla turned flips while walking on a wire high in the air. The Amazing Ricardo juggled clubs while riding a unicycle. At the end of the show, about twelve acrobats created a human pyramid.

Color in the flag that tells the main idea.

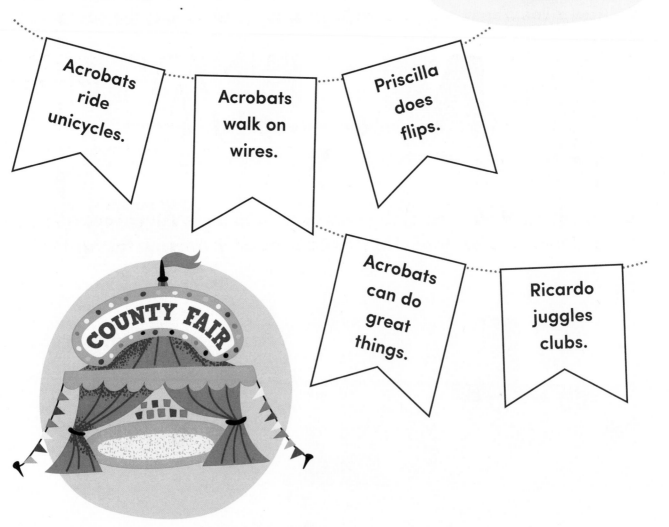

Acrobats ride unicycles.

Acrobats walk on wires.

Priscilla does flips.

Acrobats can do great things.

Ricardo juggles clubs.

Your Name

When you were born, your parents thought of a name for you. You might be named after someone in the family. Maybe you were named after a movie star! Almost every name has a meaning. *Pamela* means "honey." *Nick* means "victory of the people." *Ellen* means "bright." Sometimes books about baby names tell the meanings. Many of the meanings will surprise you!

Circle the name below that has the main idea of the text in it.

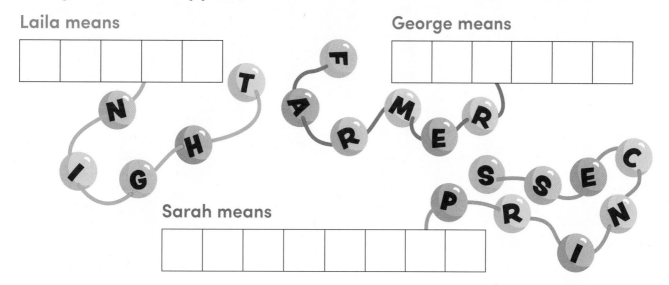

SAM — I want to be a movie star!

KATE — Names have special meanings.

To find out the meanings of the names in the puzzle below, follow each string of beads. Copy the letters on each bead in order in the boxes.

Laila means

George means

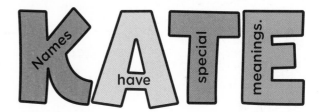

Sarah means

Striped Critters

Skunks are small animals that live in the woods. They have black fur with one or two white stripes down their backs. Bugs are their favorite food. They also eat mice. If a skunk raises its tail, run away! Skunks can spray a very smelly liquid at anyone who bothers them.

> **Details** are parts of a story. Details help you understand what the text is about.

Write the answers in the crossword puzzle.

Across:

2 What color are the stripes on a skunk's fur?

5 What is a skunk's favorite food?

Down:

1 What is another thing that skunks like to eat?

2 Where do skunks live?

3 What does a skunk raise when it is getting ready to spray?

4 What should you do if a skunk raises its tail?

Ricky's Wish

Ricky loved to go camping. One day during reading class, he began to daydream about camping in the mountains. He thought about going fishing and riding horses. It would be fun to gather logs to build a campfire and cook hot dogs. He and his dad could set up the tent near some big trees. He wished he were in his canoe right at that moment. Just then, Ricky heard his teacher say, "Ricky, it is your turn to read." Oh, no! He had lost the place!

Circle these things from the text in the picture below: a fish, a fishing pole, a log for campfire, a hot dog, a tree, and a canoe.

1 Where was Ricky during this story? _____

_____

2 Where would Ricky like to have been? _____

_____

Going to Grammy's

Kelly is going to spend the night with her grandmother. She will need to take her pajamas, a shirt, and some shorts. Into the suitcase go her toothbrush, toothpaste, and hairbrush. Grammy told her to bring a swimsuit in case it is warm enough to swim. Mom said to pack her favorite pillow and storybooks. Dad said, "Don't forget to take Grammy's sunglasses that she left here last week." Now Kelly is ready to go!

1 Color the things that Kelly packed in her suitcase.

2 A compound word is a big word that is made up of two little words. For example, cow + boy = cowboy. Find 8 compound words in this story and circle them.

 On another sheet of paper, make a list of things you would pack if you were going to spend the night at your grandmother's house.

George W. Bush

George W. Bush grew up in Texas. When he finished college, he worked in the oil business. Later on, he became the governor of Texas, then the 43rd president of the United States. His wife's name is Laura. They have twin daughters named Jenna and Barbara. The Bush family owns a ranch in Texas. They had two dogs named Barney and Spotty.

The Bush family also had a cat. To find out the name of their cat, write the answers in the blanks. Then copy the letters that are in the shapes into the empty shapes below.

1 Mr. Bush grew up in ____ ____ ____ ____ ____ .

2 He worked in the ____ ____ ____ business.

3 He became the 43rd ____ ____ ____ ____ ____ ____ ____ of the United States.

4 Laura Bush is Mr. Bush's ____ ____ ____ ____ .

5 His daughters' names are Barbara and ____ ____ ____ ____ ____ .

His cat's name was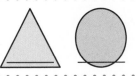

Mr. Lee's Store

At night, Mr. Lee locked the store and went home. That's when the fun began! The ketchup bottles stood in rows like bowling pins. Then, the watermelon rolled down the aisle and knocked them down. The chicken wings flew around the room. Cans of soup stacked themselves higher and higher until they laughed so hard that they tumbled over. Carrots danced with bananas. Then it was

morning. "Get back in your places!" called the milk jug. "Mr. Lee is coming!" Mr. Lee opened the door and went right to work.

Circle the cans that are fantasy.

Mr. Lee went home at night.

a talking milk jug

dancing bananas

laughing soup cans

Mr. Lee went to work.

chicken wings that can fly all by themselves

ketchup bottles and a watermelon bowling

dancing carrots

a grocery store

Cool Clouds

Have you ever looked up in the sky and seen a
cloud that is shaped like an animal or a person?
Big, white, puffy clouds float along like soft
marshmallows. In cartoons, people can sit on
clouds and bounce on them. But clouds are really just tiny drops of
water floating in the air. You can understand what being in a cloud
is like when it is foggy. Fog is a cloud near the ground!

**Read each sentence below. If the sentence could really happen,
color the cloud blue. If the sentence is fantasy, color it orange.**

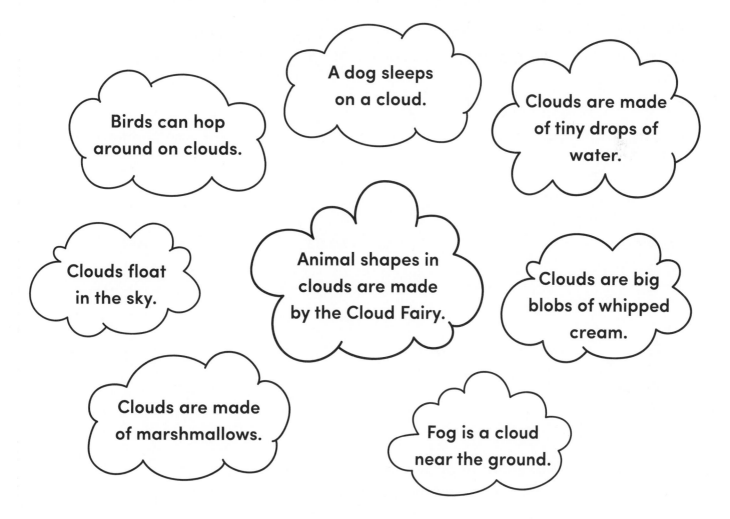

Birds can hop
around on clouds.

A dog sleeps
on a cloud.

Clouds are made
of tiny drops of
water.

Clouds float
in the sky.

Animal shapes in
clouds are made
by the Cloud Fairy.

Clouds are big
blobs of whipped
cream.

Clouds are made
of marshmallows.

Fog is a cloud
near the ground.

Fun at the Farm

Read each sentence below. If it could be real, circle the picture.
If it is fantasy, put an X on the picture.

 Dairy cows give milk.

 Four little ducks swam in the pond.

 The pig said, "Let's go to the dance tonight!"

 The farmer planted pizza and sandwiches.

 The hay was stacked in the barn.

 The mouse ate the dinner table.

 The green tractor ran out of gas.

 The chicken laid golden eggs.

 The goat and the sheep got married by the big tree.

 Rain made the roads muddy.

 Horses sat on the couch and watched TV.

 The farmer baked a pumpkin pie.

 On another sheet of paper, write one make-believe sentence about the farmer's house and one real sentence about it.

Ready for School

To **sequence** means putting the events in a story in the order they happened.

Tara could hardly wait for school to start. Mom drove her to the store to buy school supplies. They bought pencils, crayons, scissors, and glue. When Tara got home, she wrote her name on all her supplies. She put them in a paper sack. The next day, Tara went to school, but the principal told her and the other children to go back home. A water leak had flooded the building. Oh, no! Tara would have to wait another whole week!

Number the pictures in the order that they happened in the story.

Color the supplies that Tara bought.

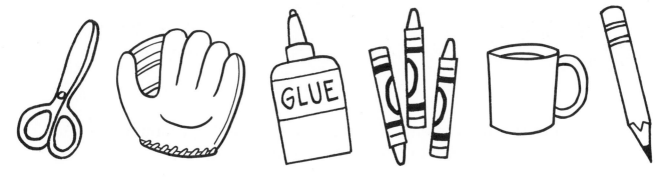

Swimming Lessons

Last summer, I learned how to swim. First, the teacher told me to hold my breath. Then, I learned to put my head under water. I practiced kicking my feet. While I held on to a float, I paddled around the pool. Next, I paddled to my teacher. Finally, I swam using both my arms and legs. I did it! Swimming is fun! This summer, I want to learn to dive off the diving board.

Number the pictures in the order that they happened in the story.

Unscramble the letters to tell what the person in the story wants to do next.

  EALNR   **OT**   **IVDE**

_____   _____   _____

 What would you like to learn to do? Draw four pictures on another sheet of paper to show how to do it.

Shapes in the Sky

Follow the directions.

1 Outline each star with a blue crayon. Then color each one red.

2 Color one moon yellow. Color the other one orange.

3 Draw a face on every sun.

4 Write the number of stars inside the star.

5 Write the number of moons inside the moon.

6 Write the number of suns inside the sun.

7 Add the three numbers you wrote together

to find the total number of shapes. _____ + _____ + _____ = _____

8 Which two shapes belong in the night sky?

_____ and _____

Scholastic Success With Reading Comprehension • Grade 1   **17**

My Monster

Read the story.

I saw a scary monster that lived in a cave. It had shaggy fur and a long, striped tail. It had ugly, black teeth. Its three horns were shaped like arrows. One of its feet was bigger than the other three. "Wake up! Time for breakfast," Mom said. Oh, good! It was only a dream.

Read the directions below carefully. Follow the directions. Look for key words such as *circle,* *underline,* **and** *draw.*

1 What did the monster's tail look like? Circle it.

2 What did the monster's horns look like? Circle them.

3 What did the monster's feet look like? Underline them.

4 Which of these is the correct picture of the monster?
Draw a cave around it.

Fun at the Beach

Jack and Joni went to the beach today. Mom spread a blanket on the sand, and they had a picnic. It got very hot, so Jack and Joni jumped into the cold water. They climbed into a big yellow raft. The waves made the raft go up and down. Later, they played in the sand and built sandcastles. Jack and Joni picked up pretty shells. Joni found a sea star. What a fun day!

1 Color the pictures below that are from the story.
Put an X on the ones that don't belong.

2 In the third sentence, find two words that are opposites of each other and circle them with a red crayon.

3 What color was the raft? Show your answer by coloring the picture at the top of the page.

My New Rug

I bought a fancy rug today. It was made of brightly colored yarn. I placed it on the floor in front of the TV and sat on it. All of a sudden, it lifted me up in the air! The rug and I flew around the house. Then out the door we went. High above the trees, we soared like eagles. Finally, it took me home, and we landed in my backyard.

How could that have happened? To find out, use your crayons to trace over each line. Use a different color on each line. Write the letter from that line in the box at the bottom of the rug.

T A I S W F I A L N Y A R G C T P E

Could this story really happen? Draw a rug around your answer.

Yes   No

Polly Want a Cracker?

Have you ever heard a parrot talk? Parrots are able to copy sounds that they hear. You can train a parrot to repeat words, songs, and whistles. But a parrot cannot say words that it has never heard. People can use words to make new sentences, but most parrots cannot.

Read each sentence. If it is true, color the parrot under True. If it is false, color the parrot under False.

	True	**False**
1 You can teach a parrot to sing "Happy Birthday."		
2 You can ask a parrot any question, and it could give you an answer.		
3 A parrot can make up a fairy tale.		
4 If a parrot heard your mom say "Brush your teeth" every night, he could learn to say it, too.		
5 It is possible for a parrot to repeat words in Spanish.		

You Be the Artist

Artists drew the pictures that are in this book. Now it is your turn to be the artist! Read each sentence very carefully. Draw exactly what you read about in the sentence.

Picturing a story can help the reader understand it better.

1 The green and yellow striped snake wiggled past the ants.

2 Wildflowers grew along the banks of the winding river.

3 On her sixth birthday, Shannon had a pink birthday cake shaped like a butterfly.

A Stormy Day

Read the story below. Then go back and read each sentence again. Add to the picture everything that the sentences describe.

Big black clouds appeared in the sky. Lightning struck the tallest tree. The scared cow cried, "Moo!" It rained hard. Soon there was a mud puddle by the barn door. Hay blew out of the barn window.

Who Am I?

Circle the picture that answers the riddle.

Use details from the sentences to decide which character each riddle describes.

1 I have feathers, I also have wings, but I don't fly. I love to swim in icy water. Who am I?

2 I live in the ocean. I swim around looking for something to eat. I have six more arms than you have. Who am I?

3 I like to watch movies and listen to music. My grandchildren love my oatmeal cookies. Who am I?

4 I am an insect. If you touch me, I might bite you! I make tunnels under the ground. I love to come to your picnic! Who am I?

What's Going On?

James was the first boy in Miss Lane's class to start feeling itchy. His scalp became so itchy that his mom came to take him home. The next day, Amy and Jana started feeling itchy, too. The next Monday, six more children were absent. Finally, everyone got well and came back to school. But this time, Miss Lane was absent. Guess what was wrong with her!

Circle the correct answers.

1 What do you think was wrong with the children?

○ headache   ○ head lice   ○ broken arms

2 How do you know?

○ The children had itchy scalps.   ○ The children came back to school.

3 How many children in all had this problem?

4 Why do you think Miss Lane was absent? Write your answer.

_____

_____

Make a Cartoon

Read the sentences below each picture.
In the bubbles, write what each character could be saying.

Mr. Giraffe asked Mr. Zebra why he had stripes. Mr. Zebra didn't know.

Mr. Giraffe said that he should ask Mrs. Owl. Mr. Zebra agreed.

Mr. Zebra asked Mrs. Owl why he had stripes. Mrs. Owl laughed.

Mrs. Owl told Mr. Zebra that the Magic Fairy painted him that way!

Clean Your Room

Mom says, "Let's go out for ice cream! Clean your room, and then we will go." Your room is a mess. You need to put the blocks in the basket. The crayons must go in their box. The books must go on the shelf, and the marbles go in the jar. You can do it. Just think about that hot fudge sundae!

> Grouping like things together makes it easier to remember what you need.

Draw a line from each item on the floor to where it belongs. Color what you could use in school green. Color toys blue.

Circle the food that does not belong in an ice cream store.

Going to the Mall

Read the words in the Word Bank. Write each word in the place where you would find these items at the mall.

Word Bank

tickets	sandals	tacos	beans	big screen
tulip bulbs	peppers	fertilizer	popcorn	soil
sneakers	burritos	boots	shovel	candy

Sadie's Shoe Store

_____

_____

_____

_____

Pepe's Mexican Food

_____

_____

_____

_____

MOVIE TOWN CINEMA

_____

_____

_____

_____

GARDEN SHOP

_____

_____

_____

My Favorites

This page is all about you!
Read the categories and write your own answers.

My Favorite TV Shows	My Favorite Foods	My Favorite Sports
_____	_____	_____
_____	_____	_____
_____	_____	_____

Draw two of your favorite people here and write their names.

Favorite Color

_____

Favorite Holiday

_____

Favorite Song

_____

Favorite Movie

_____

Favorite School Subject

_____

Favorite Thing to Do With My Family

_____

Ouch!

Mia and Rosa were playing hospital. Mia was the patient, and Rosa was the doctor. Rosa pretended to take Mia's temperature. "You have a fever," she said. "You will have to lie down." Mia climbed onto the top bunk bed. "You need to sleep," Dr. Rosa said. Mia rolled over too far and fell off the top bunk. "O-o-o-h, my arm!" yelled Mia. Her mother came to look. It was broken!

What do you think happened next? Write your answer here.

_____

To find out if your answer is correct, finish the sentence below by coloring only the spaces that have a dot in them.

Mia had to go to

What Will Sam Do?

One day, Sam was riding his bike to the baseball game. He had to be on time. He was the pitcher. Just ahead, Sam saw a little boy who had fallen off his bike. His knee was bleeding, and he was crying. Sam asked him if he was okay, but the boy couldn't speak. Sam knew the boy needed help getting home. If he stopped to help, he might be late for the game. Sam thought about it. He knew he had to do the right thing.

What will Sam do next? There are two paths through the maze. Draw a line along the path that shows what you think Sam did next.

Which sentence from the story gives you a hint about what Sam decided to do? Write the sentence below.

_____

_____

Riddle Fun

To solve the riddles in each box, answer the questions to find letter clues. Then write the letters in the blanks with the matching numbers.

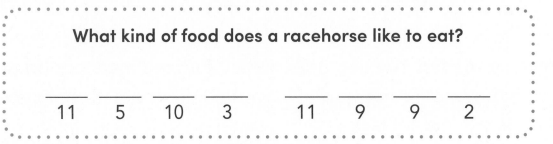

What kind of food does a racehorse like to eat?

___ ___ ___ ___   ___ ___ ___ ___
11   5   10   3   11   9   9   2

1. What letter is in **LOG**, but not in **DOG**?

2. What letter is in **DIME**, but not in **TIME**?

3. What letter is in **BITE**, but not in **BIKE**?

4. What letter is in **WEST**, but not in **REST**?

5. What letter is in **FAN**, but not in **FUN**?

6. What letter is in **BOX**, but not in **FOX**?

7. What letter is in **CAR**, but not in **CAN**?

8. What letter is in **ME**, but not in **MY**?

9. What letter is in **SOCK**, but not in **SACK**?

10. What letter is in **SEE**, but not in **BEE**?

11. What letter is in **FULL**, but not in **PULL**?

What does a rose sleep in at night?

___ ___ ___ ___ ___ ___   ___ ___ ___
11   1   9   4   8   7   6   8   2

Twins

Holly and Polly are twins. They are in the first grade. They look alike, but they are very different. Holly likes to play softball and soccer. She likes to wear her hair braided when she goes out to play. She wears sporty clothes. Recess is her favorite part of school. Polly likes to read books and paint pictures. Every day she wears a ribbon in her hair to match her dress. Her favorite thing about school is going to the library. She wants to be a teacher some day.

Look at the pictures of Holly and Polly. They look alike, but there are differences. Can you find them? Circle the things that are different.

Underline the sentence that tells what is the same about Holly and Polly.

They play sports.   They love to paint.   They are in the first grade.

Soldier Moms

Juan's mother and Ann's mother are soldiers. Juan's mother is a captain in the Navy. She sails on the ocean in a large ship. Ann's mother is a pilot in the Air Force. She flies a jet. Juan and Ann miss their moms when they are gone for a long time. They write them letters and send them pictures. It is a happy day when their moms come home!

Draw a ☺ in the column under the correct mom.
Some sentences may describe both moms.

	Juan's mom	Ann's mom	Both moms
She is a captain.			
She works on a ship.			
Sometimes she is gone for a long time.			
She is a pilot.			
Her child writes to her.			
She is in the Air Force.			
She is in the Navy.			
It is a happy time when she comes home.			
She flies a jet.			
She is a soldier.			

Dinosaur Clues

How do we know that dinosaurs were real? It is because their bones have been found in rocks. Scientists have found dinosaur footprints where mud later turned to stone. These kinds of rocks are called **fossils**. Fossils give us clues about how big the dinosaurs were. Some were small and some were very large. Scientists say a diplodocus was about as big as three school buses!

1 Color the picture that shows scientists working.

2 Color the picture of a fossil.

 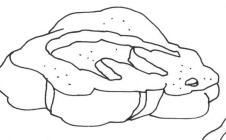 

3 Color the picture of a diplodocus.

Amazing Animal Facts

Read each sentence. Then fill in the circle that tells the meaning of the underlined word.

1. Sea lions sometimes sleep in the water with one <u>flipper</u> up in the air.
   - ○ an arm like a paddle
   - ○ a beak
   - ○ a feather

2. Even though whale sharks are the biggest fish in the world, they are <u>harmless</u> to people.
   - ○ reddish brown
   - ○ not dangerous
   - ○ very tiny

3. Horses use their tails to <u>swat</u> pesky flies.
   - ○ slap at
   - ○ catch
   - ○ eat

4. Snakes <u>shed</u> their old skins and grow new ones.
   - ○ comb
   - ○ burn
   - ○ lose

5. Squirrels <u>bury</u> acorns and nuts to eat when winter comes.
   - ○ bake
   - ○ hide in the ground
   - ○ search for

A Tiny Town

Have you ever seen a prairie dog town? That's where the <u>prairie dogs</u> live, but there are no buildings or houses. They live underground. They dig deep into the dirt making <u>burrows</u>. Along the burrows, here and there, are <u>chambers</u> for sleeping or storing food. One chamber is lined with grass for the babies. Sometimes prairie dogs have <u>unwanted</u> <u>guests</u> in their town, like rattlesnakes!

Use the code below to learn what some of the words in the story mean. Copy the matching letters in the blanks.

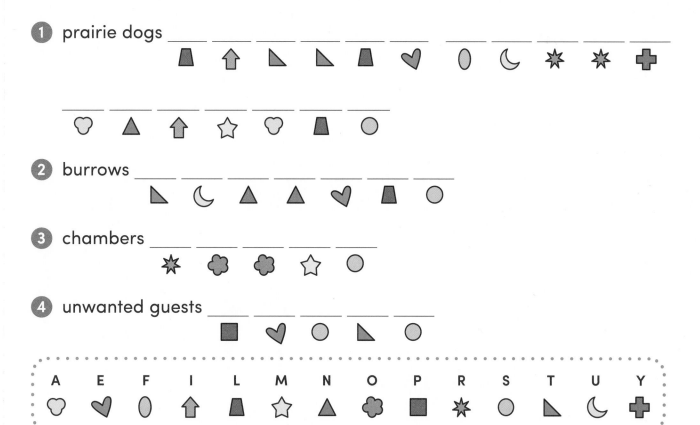

1 prairie dogs ____ ____ ____ ____ ____ ____ ____ ____ ____ ____ ____

____ ____ ____ ____ ____ ____ ____

2 burrows ____ ____ ____ ____ ____ ____ ____

3 chambers ____ ____ ____ ____ ____

4 unwanted guests ____ ____ ____ ____ ____

Oops!

Sandy went on a vacation in the mountains with her parents and little brother, Austin. They were staying in a small cabin without any electricity or running water. It was fun to have lanterns at night and to bathe in the cold mountain stream. The biggest problem for Sandy was she missed her best friend, Kendra. Sandy found her dad's cell phone and called Kendra. They talked for nearly an hour! When Sandy's dad went to call his office, the cell phone was dead. He was NOT a happy camper!

> In a story, there is usually a reason something happens. This is the **cause**. What happens as a result is the **effect**.

Draw a line to match the first part of each sentence to the second part that makes it true.

1. Sandy used lanterns at night because

2. Sandy and Austin bathed in a stream because

3. Sandy felt better about missing Kendra because

4. Sandy's dad could not call his office because

the cell phone was dead.

she talked to her on the cell phone.

the cabin had no running water.

the cabin had no electricity.

 Write about something you did that caused a huge "effect."

Wanda Wiggleworm

Wanda Wiggleworm was tired of living alone in the flowerpot, so she decided to go out and meet other worms. Last night, Wanda went to the Bug Ball. She looked her best, all slick and slippery. Carl Caterpillar asked her to dance. They wiggled around and around to the music. All of a sudden they got tangled up. They tried to get free, but instead, they tied themselves in a knot! What did they do? They decided to get married and live happily ever after.

Unscramble each sentence about the text.
Write the new sentence on the lines below.

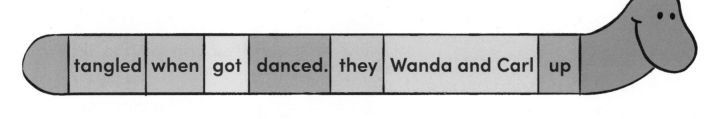

| tangled | when | got | danced. | they | Wanda and Carl | up |

_____

_____

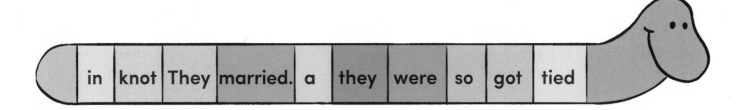

| in | knot | They | married. | a | they | were | so | got | tied |

_____

_____

School Rules

It is important to follow the rules at school. Read each rule below. Find the picture that shows what could happen if students DID NOT follow that rule. Write the letter of the picture in the correct box.

1 You must walk, not run, in the halls.

2 Do not chew gum at school.

3 Come to school on time.

4 When the fire alarm rings, follow the leader outside.

5 Listen when the teacher is talking.

6 Keep your desk clean.

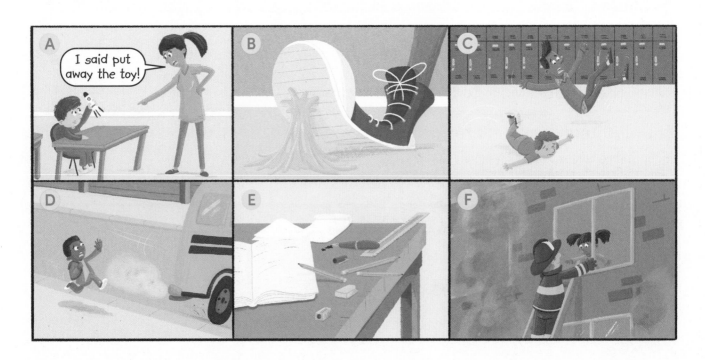

Mixed-Up Margie

Once upon a time, there was a mixed-up queen named Margie. She got things mixed up. She wore her crown on her arm. She wore a shoe on her head. She painted her nose red! She used a fork to hold her hair in place. She wore a purple belt around her knees. The king didn't mind. He always wore his clothes backward!

> A **character** is a person or animal in a story. To help readers understand a character better, a story often gives details about the character.

Use the story and your crayons to help you follow these instructions:

1 Draw Margie a crown.

2 Draw her shoe.

3 Paint her nose.

4 Draw what goes in her hair.

5 Draw her belt.

Fill in the bubble next to the correct answer.

1 What makes you think Margie is mixed up?
○ the way she dresses
○ the way she talks

2 What makes you think the king is mixed up, too?
○ He talks backward.
○ He wears his clothes backward.

Miss Ticklefoot

I love Miss Ticklefoot. She is my first-grade teacher.

To find out more about her, read each sentence below. Write a word in each blank that tells how she feels. Use the words in the Word Bank.

Word Bank

| sad | scared | silly | worried | happy | surprised |

1 Miss Ticklefoot smiles when we know the answers.

_____

2 She is concerned when one of us is sick.

_____

3 She makes funny faces at us during recess.

_____

4 She cried when our fish died.

_____

5 She jumps when the fire alarm rings.

_____

6 Her mouth dropped open when we gave her a present!

_____

Different Friends

When Ty was four years old, he had two make-believe friends named Mr. Go-Go and Mr. Sasso. When there was no one else around, Ty talked to Mr. Go-Go while he played with his toys. Mr. Go-Go was a good friend. He helped put Ty's toys away. Mr. Sasso was not a good friend. Some days he forgot to make Ty's bed or brush Ty's teeth. Another day, Dad said, "Oh, my! Who wrote on the wall?" Ty knew who did it... Mr. Sasso!

Read the phrase inside each crayon. If it describes Mr. Go-Go, color it green. If it describes Mr. Sasso, color it red. If it describes both, color it yellow.

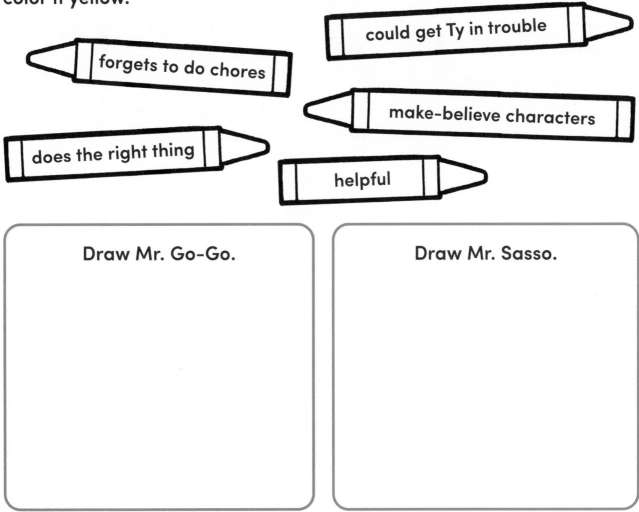

could get Ty in trouble

forgets to do chores

make-believe characters

does the right thing

helpful

Draw Mr. Go-Go.

Draw Mr. Sasso.

Poetry

A **poem** paints a picture with words. It often uses rhyming words.

Colorful Sky
When thunderstorms are near
Colored strips appear.
At the end, I'm told
There'll be a pot of gold.

Draw what it is.

1 Draw a red line under the word that rhymes with **near**.

2 Draw a green line under the word that rhymes with **told**.

What's That in the Sky?
It flies up in the sky.
It takes you way up high.
You see an airport, then
It takes you down again.

Draw what it is.

3 Draw a blue circle around the word that rhymes with **sky**.

4 Draw a brown circle around the word that rhymes with **then**.

5 Finish the two-line poem below:

I wish that I could see

A giant bumble _____.

Draw what it is.

A Fable

A **fable** is a story that teaches a lesson. This fable was written many, many years ago.

The Dog and His Shadow

A dog carried a piece of meat in his mouth. He crossed over a river on a low bridge. He looked down into the water and saw his reflection. It looked like another dog with a piece of meat larger than his. The dog snapped at the other dog's meat. When he did, his own meat dropped into the water. Now the dog didn't have any meat at all.

Draw a box around the lesson that the story teaches:

1 Two dogs are better than one.

2 Don't be greedy. Be happy with what you have.

Color only the pictures of things that you read about in the story:

 Write a complete sentence telling what the dog should have done.

Library Books

A library has many different kinds of books. Have you ever read *The Rainbow Fish* by Marcus Pfister? It is a story about a very special fish. His scales were blue, green, and purple. He also had some shiny silver scales. The other fish wanted him to share his shiny scales with them, but he said no. No one would be his friend. Later, he decided to give each fish one of his shiny scales. It was better to lose some of his beauty and have friends than to keep the scales to himself.

Connect the dots. You will see something from the book.

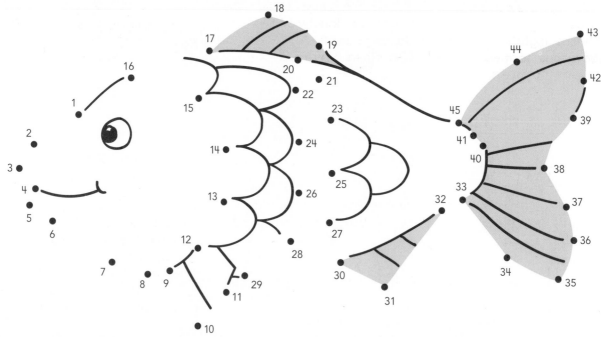

1 Which word tells what this book is about? Fill in the circle.

○ running   ○ lying   ○ sharing   ○ eating

2 Write the name of the author here.

_____

ANSWER KEY

Page 5
Main idea: Trucks do important work.

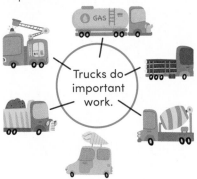

Trucks do important work.

Page 6
Main idea: Acrobats can do great things.

Page 7
KATE: Names have special meanings.
Laila means "night."
George means "farmer."
Sarah means "princess."

Page 8

				m		
				i		
				c		
w	h	i	t	e		
o				a		
o				i		
r		d		l		
b	u	g	s			
n						

Page 9

1. in reading class 2. camping

Page 10
Kelly packed pajamas, shirt, shorts, toothbrush, toothpaste, hairbrush, swimsuit, pillow, storybooks, sunglasses.
Compound words: grandmother, suitcase, toothbrush, toothpaste, hairbrush, swimsuit, storybooks, sunglasses

Page 11
1. Texas 2. oil 3. president
4. wife 5. Jenna
His cat's name was INDIA.

Page 12
Fantasy: ketchup bottles and a watermelon bowling, a talking milk jug, dancing bananas, chicken wings that can fly all by themselves, laughing soup cans, dancing carrots
(The others are real.)

Page 13
Facts: Clouds float in the sky. Clouds are made of tiny drops of water. Fog is a cloud near the ground. (All others are fantasy.)

Page 14
Fantasy: pig, goat and sheep, horses, pizza and sandwiches, mouse, golden eggs
(The others are real.)

Page 15
5, 4, 3, 1, 2
Tara bought pencils, scissors, glue, and crayons.

Page 16
6, 4, 2; 3, 1, 5; LEARN TO DIVE

Page 17
1. Each star should be outlined in blue and colored red inside.
2. One moon should be yellow and one orange.
3. A face should be drawn on each sun.
4. 3 5. 2 6. 4 7. 3 + 2 + 4 = 9
8. stars and moons

Page 18

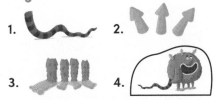

Page 19
1. The pictures that do not belong are pumpkin, snowman, frog, and skates. (The other pictures should be colored.)
2. hot, cold 3. yellow

Page 20
IT WAS A FLYING CARPET.
No

Page 21
1. true 2. false 3. false
4. true 5. true

Page 22
Pictures should include everything described in the sentences.

Page 23
The following should have been added to the picture: black clouds, lightning striking the tallest tree, the word "Moo" in a bubble above a cow, rain, a mud puddle by the barn door, hay blowing out of the barn window

Page 24
1. penguin 2. octopus
3. grandmother 4. ant

Page 25
1. head lice
2. The children had itchy scalps.
3. 9 4. She got head lice, too.

Page 26

Page 27

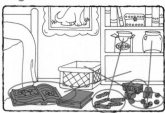

The hamburger does not belong.

Page 28

Sadie's Shoe Store: sandals, boots, sneakers
Movie Town Cinema: tickets, popcorn, big screen, candy
Pepe's Mexican Food: tacos, burritos, beans, peppers
Garden Shop: tulip bulbs, fertilizer, shovel, soil

Page 29

Answers will vary.

Page 30

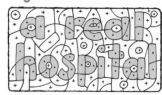

Page 31

He knew he had to do the right thing.

Page 32

FAST FOOD, FLOWER BED

Page 33

Same: They are in the first grade.

Page 34

Juan's mother: She is a captain. She works on a ship. She is in the Navy.
Ann's mother: She is a pilot. She is in the Air Force. She flies a jet. (The other sentences apply to both mothers.)

Page 35

1.
2.
3.

Page 36

1. an arm like a paddle
2. not dangerous 3. slap at
4. lose 5. hide in the ground

Page 37

1. little furry animals 2. tunnels
3. rooms 4. pests

Page 38

1. Sandy used lanterns at night because the cabin had no electricity.
2. Sandy and Austin bathed in a stream because the cabin had no running water.
3. Sandy felt better about missing Kendra because she talked to her on the cell phone.

4. Sandy's dad could not call his office because the cell phone was dead.

Page 39

1. Wanda and Carl got tangled up when they danced.
2. They were tied in a knot so they got married.

Page 40

1. C 2. B 3. D 4. F 5. A 6. E

Page 41

Pictures should show a crown on Margie's arm, a shoe on her head, a red nose, a fork in her hair, and a purple belt around her knees.
1. the way she dresses
2. He wears his clothes backward.

Page 42

1. happy 2. worried 3. silly
4. sad 5. scared 6. surprised

Page 43

Green: helpful, does the right thing **Red:** forgets to do chores, could get Ty in trouble
Yellow: make-believe characters

Page 44

Picture: rainbow 1. appear
2. gold Picture: airplane
3. high 4. again 5. bee

Page 45

2. Don't be greedy. Be happy with what you have.
Color: dog, meat, bridge

Page 46

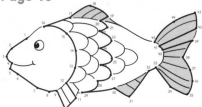

1. sharing 2. Marcus Pfister